ALBERT SCHWEITZER

Other titles in the
PEOPLE WHO MADE A DIFFERENCE
series include

Louis Braille
Marie Curie
Father Damien
Mahatma Gandhi
Bob Geldof
Martin Luther King, Jr.
Ralph Nader
Florence Nightingale
Mother Teresa
Sojourner Truth
Desmond Tutu

North American edition first published in 1991 by
Gareth Stevens Children's Books
1555 North RiverCenter Drive, Suite 201
Milwaukee, Wisconsin 53212, USA

This edition is abridged from *Albert Schweitzer: The doctor who gave up a brilliant career to serve the people of Africa,* copyright © 1988 by Exley Publications Ltd. and written by James Bentley. Additional end matter copyright © 1991 by Gareth Stevens, Inc.
All rights reserved. No part of this book may be reproduced in any form or by any means without permission in writing from Gareth Stevens, Inc.

Library of Congress Cataloging-in-Publication Data

Lantier, Patricia, 1952-
    Albert Schweitzer / Patricia Lantier's adaptation of the book by James Bentley. — North American ed.
        p.   cm. — (People who made a difference)
    Includes index.
    Summary: Examines the life of the humanitarian who pursued medical missionary work in the jungles of Africa while developing his spiritual beliefs about the value of all life.
    ISBN 0-8368-0457-0
    1. Schweitzer, Albert, 1875-1965—Juvenile literature. 2. Strasbourg (France)—Biography—Juvenile literature. 3. Missionaries, Medical—Gabon—Lambaréné (Moyen-Ogooué)—Biography—Juvenile literature. 4. Theologians—Europe—Biography—Juvenile literature. 5. Musicians—Europe—Biography—Juvenile literature. [1. Schweitzer, Albert, 1875-1965. 2. Missionaries. 3. Physicians.] I. Bentley, James, 1937- Albert Schweitzer. II. Title. III. Series.
CT1018.S45L36   1990   610'.92—dc20
[B]   [92]   90-9974

For a free color catalog describing Gareth Stevens' list of high-quality children's books, call

**1-800-341-3569 (USA) or
1-800-461-9120 (Canada)**

PICTURE CREDITS
Albert Schweitzer Archives, Günsbach, France — 7, 12-13, 14, 17, 18, 20, 21, 24, 32-33, 34 (both), 35, 52; © Erica Anderson photographs by courtesy of the Albert Schweitzer Center, Great Barrington, Massachusetts 01230, USA [telephone (413) 528-3124] — 4, 8, 10, 11, 23, 28, 29, 37, 42, 43, 44, 46, 47, 48, 49, 53, 54, 56, 58, 59; Ardea — 40; Bildarchiv Prussicher Kulturbesitz — 27; GSF Picture Library — 31; Keystone Collection — 55; Popperfoto — Tom Redman — cover illustration; Topham Picture Library — 15.

Map drawn by Geoffrey Pleasance.

Exley Publications would particularly like to thank Mrs. Vreni Mark, director of the Albert Schweitzer Archive in Günsbach, and Dr. Kathleen Collins, archivist of the Albert Schweitzer Center in Massachusetts, for their invaluable help in obtaining pictures for this book and for additional information about Dr. Schweitzer in later years.

Series conceived and edited by Helen Exley
Series editor, U.S.: Amy Bauman
Editorial assistants, U.S.: Scott Enk, Diane Laska, John D. Ratcliff
Cover design: Kate Kriege

Printed in the United States of America

1 2 3 4 5 6 7 8 9 95 94 93 92 91

PEOPLE
WHO MADE
A DIFFERENCE

*The doctor
who devoted
his life to
Africa's sick*

ALBERT SCHWEITZER

**Patricia
Lantier**

**James
Bentley**

Gareth Stevens Children's Books
MILWAUKEE

A hospital in the jungle

It is 1913. A German doctor is operating on black patients in the African jungle. His hospital there is a tiny but clean chicken coop. A black assistant cleans the doctor's instruments by putting them into boiling water. The doctor's wife helps too, giving the patients medicine to put them to sleep. Outside, the patients' relatives sit quietly on the ground. They hope that their loved ones can be cured by this strange white man.

This doctor would become one of the most famous men of the century. He was a musician, a student of religion, and a writer. He was also a doctor who gave hope to the poor, sick people of Africa. His name was Albert Schweitzer.

Terrible diseases

Schweitzer's job was not an easy one. Africa's hot, wet climate caused many of the diseases. Some common problems he came across included malaria, sleeping sickness, ulcers, leprosy, and skin diseases. The people also suffered from snakebites

"Schweitzer. He is one of the personalities of this century who has become almost a myth. His sacrificial work in Africa ... established him as a saint in the minds of millions. His compassion for the animal kingdom, his creation of a jungle hospital, his plea for international understanding amid a global arms race — all seemed to set him apart from common humanity."
George Marshall and David Poling, in Schweitzer: A Biography

Opposite: Albert Schweitzer returns to his hospital in Gabon, in Africa, from a visit to Europe. Years earlier Schweitzer had read about the suffering people in Africa. He devoted the next fifty years working to build his jungle hospital at Lambaréné.

5

and attacks by wild animals. And sometimes the patients made their problems worse themselves by bathing in dirty water or touching their wounds under the bandages.

Albert Schweitzer's patients

Dr. Schweitzer faced many such problems. But he loved his work, and word of him and his work spread quickly. Soon patients were coming from all around for the doctor's help. Some people walked more than 200 miles (320 km). Often these patients arrived too thin and too weak to be helped right away. Then the doctor and his helpers would have to nurse them for several weeks. Only then were they healthy enough for the doctor to operate on them.

The African people believed in the work done at the jungle hospital. Albert Schweitzer treated nearly two thousand natives in the first nine months there. By the 1940s, at least five thousand patients came to the hospital every year.

The patients knew exactly what they wanted from the jungle doctor. One story tells how one of Schweitzer's doctors tried to cheer up a patient before she had an operation. He talked to her for a few minutes. She ignored him. He continued talking. Finally, she interrupted him, saying, "This is no time for gossip. You should cut."

Albert Schweitzer ran his jungle hospital for fifty years. Only poor health and World War I kept him from his duties there. During these years, he gained the respect of the African people. Many saw him as a saint. By day, he was a doctor who saved countless lives. By night, he was a writer whose books on philosophy and religion reached people throughout the world.

Patients at Schweitzer's first jungle hospital sit in the open air and wait to be treated. Patients were treated free. Those who could afford it often paid with chickens, eggs, or some other food.

Answering his critics
People did not always understand Albert Schweitzer. For example, by the end of 1913, he had built a new hospital to

The hospital at Lambaréné was an informal place, with children wandering around happily and patients sitting outside wherever they wished. It was always crowded. Meanwhile, the large, white hospitals such as those found in Europe had few patients.

replace the old chicken coop. But some people criticized the new hospital because it did not have all the most modern equipment.

But Schweitzer knew that this was the kind of hospital to build for the African people. Until this time, the people had been going to witch doctors when they were sick. Witch doctors used charms and potions to cure their patients.

Schweitzer knew that if he wanted the African people to come to him for help, his new hospital would have to please them. It could not look too strange to them. So he knew he could not build a modern clinic.

So Schweitzer's hospital looked like an African village. Long rows of huts stood side by side. Each patient had a hut, and his or her entire family stayed there, too. Only the operating room had electricity, so the people cooked on small burners outside. Animals moved freely around the entire area.

This felt like home to the local people. They would not have liked a modern hospital with big, white buildings and strange machines. But visitors were often shocked. Many expected to see a hospital like those in Europe.

Schweitzer's hospital was very successful. It grew to more than seventy rows of huts, and the doctors and nurses treated up to six hundred patients a day. Over the years, medical people from all over the world came to Africa to help at the clinic.

"He had a real understanding of when a man was sick. . . . When he was just causing the man more misery he would instinctively feel it. He could tell when a man was near death. . . . I can remember him ordering me to incise a big abscess sometimes when I thought I'd just wait another day. He'd say: 'No, now, today, this minute, you must incise it today, no more delay.' And he was right, every time. There would be a pint or two of pus in this man's leg — these big tropical abscesses."
Frank Catchpool,
one of Lambaréné's doctors

Africa changes

Africa went through many changes during the time that Albert Schweitzer worked there. The island area in which the hospital stood was known as Lambaréné. This was originally part of a French colony. Eventually, this colony became the Republic of Gabon.

The new country's leaders admired Schweitzer's work. When he died, the president of Gabon asked the people in charge of the hospital to keep the old buildings. He said the African people felt at home there.

Schweitzer becomes famous

By the late 1940s, people from all over the world had begun to notice the African hospital and Dr. Schweitzer. They admired Schweitzer's many talents and his dedication to the poor people of Africa.

In 1947, *Life* magazine called Albert Schweitzer the greatest man in the world. One day, after the article appeared, Schweitzer received a letter from the world-famous scientist Albert Einstein. Einstein wrote: "You are one of the few who combine extraordinary energy and many-sidedness with the desire to serve man and to lighten his lot." In 1955, an article about Albert Schweitzer in the *New York Times* stated that few people in history had done so much for others.

Then, in 1959, the United Nations asked the government of Gabon to choose a new member for the UN Commission on Human Rights. The president of Gabon asked Dr. Schweitzer to go. "Impossible," Schweitzer said. "My hospital needs me."

Childhood in Alsace

Albert Schweitzer was born on January 14, 1875, in Kaysersberg, a lovely town in Alsace, on the border between France

Albert Schweitzer's father was the stern, yet kindly, Pastor Louis. He first taught Albert to love music and the Bible.

and Germany. Vineyards and a ruined castle covered the hills around the town. At that time, Alsace was part of Germany, so Schweitzer was German.

Albert's parents, Louis and Adéle Schweitzer, moved to the village of Günsbach when Albert was six months old. Louis, a Protestant minister, became pastor of a small church there.

Günsbach and the area around it were very pretty. Albert loved growing up there. He spent his days wandering in the hills and valleys. Sometimes he played with friends, and sometimes he chose to play alone. As long as he was outdoors, he was happy.

Albert at school

Unfortunately, school got in the way of Albert's play. As a child, he did not like to go to school. He once said of his first day: "When on a fine October day my father for the first time put a slate under my arm and led me away to the school-mistress, I cried the whole way there."

Albert spent much of his time at school daydreaming instead of studying. His mother cried over his poor grades. But she need not have worried. As an adult, Albert Schweitzer would write books that would change the world.

The outdoors was not Albert's only interest. From a very early age, he loved music. His father had taught him to play

Schweitzer's mother was Adéle Schillinger. Her father was the pastor in a village near Kaysersberg. She and Louis met while he was assistant pastor to her father.

the church organ even before he was old enough to go to school. He first played in church for services at the age of nine. Later, when he went to school, Albert was surprised that his teacher played the organ with only one finger. He asked her why she did not play "properly," with harmony. He then showed her how to play the same song with four parts.

The teacher knew that Albert had a special talent. She urged him to practice his music. Albert saw for the first time

that he could do some things other people could not. This confused him. He was afraid that others would think he was showing off. From then on, he tried hard to hide his talent.

A sensitive boy

Even as a boy, Albert Schweitzer showed concern for other people. For example, he often worried about the poor children in Günsbach. One day, Albert playfully wrestled with a bigger boy. Albert won even though he was smaller. Angrily, the other boy pointed out that Albert won only because he ate good food every day. "If I got broth to eat twice a week, as you do, I'd be as strong as you are," the boy cried. This worried Albert. He wished he could help in some way.

At least, Albert decided, he would not wear better clothes than the other boys had to wear. They didn't have overcoats, so he wouldn't wear one. They wore clogs instead of shoes, so he did the same.

One day, his mother took him shopping

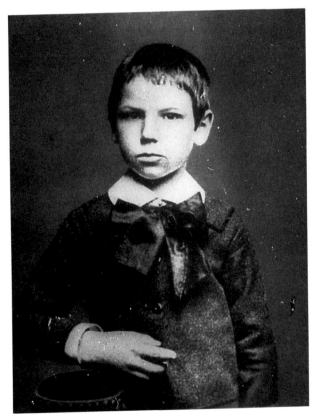

Even at seven years of age, Albert Schweitzer looked quite serious.

for a new hat. The clerk brought out a sailor's cap, but Albert would not even try it on. He wanted one like the boys at school wore. The store did not have such caps, so Albert's mother asked the clerk to order one. She did not really like the cap, but she understood how Albert felt.

Hatred of violence and suffering

At an early age, Albert began to dislike all cruelty. He especially disliked it when he saw it in himself. When he was nine or ten, he and his sister Adéle were playing a game. She was not playing well, and he angrily hit her in the face. Albert was shocked by his own cruelty.

As he grew older, Albert often sided with anyone who was hurt or mistreated. At one time, there was a poor Jewish cattle dealer who often rode through Günsbach in his cart. Each time, the village boys would chase the man, laughing at him all the way. One day, Albert saw the man turn to smile at the children. After seeing that smile, Albert never again joined in the chase.

All human suffering made Albert sad. He once said: "So far back as I can remember I was saddened by the amount of misery I saw in the world around me." The sight of suffering would often haunt him for weeks.

He felt the same way about cruelty to animals. Many of Albert's friends liked to

Albert Schweitzer was born in the Alsace region. This region is located between France and Germany. Over the centuries, Alsace has belonged to each in turn. When Albert was born in 1875, it was part of Germany.

15

hunt. One spring day, a friend suggested that he and Albert hunt for birds. Albert didn't want to go, but he did not want his friend to laugh at him. So he agreed to go. The two boys picked up their slingshots and set out. They soon spotted birds in the trees ahead and took aim. At just that moment, the church bells began to ring. Albert changed his mind about hunting and shooed the birds away.

Albert remembered that day whenever he heard church bells ring out. He remembered it because he had learned a good lesson. That day, he realized that he had to be strong to stand up for his beliefs. And after that, he often disagreed with his friends about harming animals. Even fishing bothered him. He would no longer do anything against his beliefs just so he would be accepted by other people. He did not care what anyone else thought any more.

That day also marked the start of Albert's belief in "reverence for life." This was the idea that all life is important. He would develop this belief fully while in Africa. But even now it was forming in his mind.

The church at Günsbach

Albert learned much from his early life in Günsbach. He carried some of these lessons with him all his life. One thing that he learned there was that people of

"One thing that specially saddened me was that the unfortunate animals had to suffer so much pain and misery. The sight of an old limping horse, tugged forward by one man while another kept beating it with a stick to get it to the [slaughterhouse] at Colmar, haunted me for weeks."
Albert Schweitzer

16

different beliefs could live together in peace. For many years, the Alsace area had been caught in wars between its powerful neighbors, Germany and France. These wars often started because of religious differences between Catholics and Protestants. The fighting was especially bad during the sixteenth and seventeenth centuries. Many people were hurt or killed during these conflicts.

People in Alsace no longer wanted to fight. Because of this, people learned to accept other people's religious beliefs. At Günsbach, Catholics and Protestants shared the village church. It was the same in many churches in the Alsace region.

Albert thought the church in Günsbach was beautiful. Its golden altar, tall candles, and huge statues impressed him. "When I was still merely a child," he once wrote, "I felt it to be something beautiful that in our village Catholics and Protestants worshipped in the same building."

"All my life I have been glad that I began in the village school. It was a good thing for me that in the process of learning I had to measure myself with the village boys, and thus make it quite clear to myself that they had at least as much in their heads as I had in mine."
Albert Schweitzer

Albert was always a shy person. Here, at the age of nine, he looks anxiously at the camera.

Secondary school

Albert's parents were a little better off than the other villagers of Günsbach. Still, they were not rich. They found it difficult to feed and clothe the family, which included five growing children.

Albert's parents wanted him to have the best education. But they could not afford to send him to the schools that would offer this. Luckily, Albert's great-

This photo comes from the Schweitzer family album. Schweitzer, age seventeen, sits on the left. Next to him are his brother, Pauli, his sister Margrit, a family friend, and Schweitzer's two other sisters, Adéle and Louise.

uncle Louis was able to help with this problem. Louis and his wife, Sophie, lived in the town of Mülhausen. The school there was much better than the village schools. Louis and Sophie suggested that Albert live with them and go to school in Mülhausen. Ten-year-old Albert left Günsbach unhappily.

At first, Albert did not like Mülhausen. His great-aunt and great-uncle were strict, and he missed the countryside of

Günsbach. "I felt as if I were being torn away from Nature," he wrote of leaving his village.

Albert's great-aunt may have been strict, but she was kind. She knew that Albert missed the hills of Günsbach. One sunny day, she saw him staring quietly out of the window at the melting snow. She stopped her work and asked him to take a walk with her. They walked over the canal and up the mountainside. Albert saw that his great-aunt understood how he felt. He appreciated her more from then on.

Coming out of his shell

The move to Mülhausen was not all bad. It was there that the talented and intelligent Albert Schweitzer finally showed himself. At fourteen, he suddenly found he liked school. His favorite subjects were history, science, and especially reading. He became such a hungry reader that he had trouble putting a book down once he started reading it. Sometimes he would stay up all night just to finish a book.

There, too, Albert found his love for playing the piano. He had started playing at the age of five. Now his great-aunt and great-uncle made him practice at certain times each day.   And if he finished his homework early, he practiced again in the evening.

This statue of a black man was created by Frédéric Auguste Bartholdi, who also designed the Statue of Liberty. The statue moved Schweitzer: "His face, with its sad, thoughtful expression, spoke to me of the misery of [Africa]."

His great-uncle Louis even found him a teacher named Eugen Münch. Münch was a brilliant organist from Berlin. He had come to Mülhausen to take a job as organist at St. Stephen Church.

At first, Albert found it hard to practice every day. Münch found teaching Albert just as difficult. He called the boy "a thorn in the flesh" because Albert refused to follow the lessons. Albert's problem was that he was too shy to show his teacher how well he could really play.

An inspired teacher

One day, Eugen Münch became very angry. Again, Albert had not practiced.

Münch opened a copy of *Songs Without Words*, by the German composer Felix Mendelssohn. He gave Albert the piece to practice for the next lesson. "Really you don't deserve to have such beautiful music given you to play. You'll come and spoil this . . . just like everything else," Münch said to him.

The teacher's words hurt Albert. He wanted to prove that he could play the song. So he practiced the piece again and again. At his next lesson, Albert played the finger exercises and scales carefully. Then he took a deep breath and played the Mendelssohn song for his teacher. He played with all his soul.

When Albert finished, Eugen Münch could hardly speak. He finally realized how talented Albert was. After that, Münch allowed Albert to have lessons on the church organ. Münch even trusted Albert to play the organ for the church choir. One of their songs was *Requiem* by the composer Johannes Brahms. Albert later wrote of that piece: "Then, for the first time, I knew the joy, which I have so often tasted since then, of letting the organ send the flood of its own special tones to mingle with the clanging music of the choir and orchestra."

Colmar, where Bartholdi's statue stood, was for Albert Schweitzer a glimpse of a fascinating world outside his own village. It was a world of dancing and parks, of bands and boats, of bicycles and museums, of beautiful houses and pretty girls.

Albert questions the Bible

Albert had always been interested in the Bible. The readings inspired him, and he wanted to know all about God and Jesus. But even as a boy he was puzzled by some of the things that he read in the Bible. He began asking questions about these things and was often surprised by the answers that adults gave him.

Albert once asked his father about the great flood described in the Bible. The story said that rain fell for forty days and forty nights. Water covered the whole world. One summer, it rained very much in Alsace. Albert asked his father why the water did not cover the houses as it did in the Bible story. Pastor Louis answered: "At that time, at the beginning of the world, it didn't just rain in drops, but like pouring water out of buckets."

Later, one of Albert's teachers told her class the story of the flood. Albert could hardly believe that she did not mention the great buckets of rain. "Teacher, you must tell the story correctly," he scolded.

The story of the three kings who brought gifts to Jesus also interested Albert. He had read in the Bible that Jesus' family was poor. So he wondered: "What did the parents of Jesus do . . . with the gold and other valuables which they got from these men? How could they have been poor after that?"

Music versus religion

Already in high school, Schweitzer felt torn between his two great interests. He

"Schweitzer came to survey his happiness and to wonder if it was right for him to accept it unthinkingly. On the one hand there were the warmth and tenderness of his family life, the satisfaction of work well done, the knowledge that the joys of music would grow ever more intense. And on the other, the pain and suffering of the world."

Jacques Feschotte, a friend of Schweitzer's

knew that he would go on to the University of Strasbourg when he graduated from secondary school in 1893. But he also knew that he would then have to choose to study either music or religion.

This was a hard choice to make since he loved both. He wished to become the organist of a beautiful church. But he also thought he would like to work with people and teach them about religion. Finally, he decided to spend the summer studying music in Paris and then go on to study religion and philosophy at the university.

In Paris, he met Charles-Marie Widor, a famous organist. Widor was also a teacher but accepted only the best students. Schweitzer arranged an interview with him. On the day of the interview, he arrived late. Widor was waiting impatiently for him. He asked Schweitzer what he wanted to play. Although he was shy, Albert said quickly, "Bach, of course."

No answer could have been better. Widor loved Johann Sebastian Bach's music. He listened to Schweitzer play and immediately accepted him as a pupil. In time, the two men also became friends. Throughout his life, Schweitzer often returned to Paris to study with Widor.

Schweitzer goes to the university

Schweitzer went to Strasbourg toward the end of 1893. The university there was

Schweitzer sits at the organ of St. Nicholas Church, Strasbourg. "Music gives voice to joy and sorrow, tears and laughter," he wrote, "but in such a way that it takes us from a world of unrest to a world of peace."

Schweitzer is pictured at the age of thirty-one, carrying an elegant boater hat and a cane. By this time, he was already a famous writer.

one of the best in Europe. Students were encouraged to think for themselves. It was here that Schweitzer began to question life and religion seriously.

In the middle of his studies, Schweitzer was drafted into the army. But he did not mind. He took a Greek copy of the Bible's New Testament with him when he went on training exercises and read whenever he could. The officer in charge liked Schweitzer. He tried not to make him miss classes at the university.

Schweitzer's years at the university passed quickly. He did very well, and his teachers encouraged him to continue his study of philosophy. His studies took him to universities in Paris and Berlin, where he met brilliant people.

Schweitzer returned to Strasbourg in 1899 to finish work on his philosophy degree. By this time, he was twenty-four, and he was now sure he wanted to be a preacher. He wrote: "To me, preaching was a necessity of my being." As soon as he had finished his philosophy degree, he began studying theology.

The young scholar . . .

Schweitzer stayed in Strasbourg after he graduated. He became a preacher at the Church of St. Nicholas in 1899.

Even as a preacher, Schweitzer could still be shy. Once, some members of his church told him that his sermons were too short. Schweitzer answered that he simply "stopped speaking when [he] had nothing to say."

He continued his religious studies even as a preacher. In 1903, he became the principal of Strasbourg's college of theology. There, Schweitzer's great energy gained him the respect of the people. He seemed to work all the time — as a musician, as a writer, and as a teacher. Then, after a full day's work, he would often help his students with their work.

Schweitzer had learned to work hard as a child. He always remembered the day he brought home yet another bad report card. Seeing his mother cry hurt him. "I couldn't bear to see her cry," Schweitzer said. "I took her head in my hands and kissed her and promised to work. . . . I've kept my promise."

... and organ builder

Albert Schweitzer was quickly becoming a famous student of religion. But he was also well known as a musician. At thirty, he helped start the Paris Bach Society. He spent part of each of the next eight years in Paris, playing the organ for the society's concerts. He loved this work.

Schweitzer was especially famous for his ability to play Bach's music. He had adored the composer's work from the time he was very young. Now he visited Charles-Marie Widor in Paris each spring.

> "The decision was made when I was one and twenty. In that year, while still a student, I resolved to devote my life till I was thirty to the office of preacher, to science and to music. If by that time I should have done what I hoped in science and music, I would take a path of immediate service . . . to my fellow men."
>
> *Albert Schweitzer*

Together, the great teacher and his famous student worked on the pieces of Bach's music that they loved.

Then a New York publisher asked Widor to organize all of Bach's organ music into a book. Widor said he would do the work — but only if the publisher would allow Schweitzer to help him. The publisher quickly agreed.

Soon, Schweitzer had played Bach's music on every great organ in Europe. Sadly, he found that he did not like all of these great organs. He said that many of them could not carry the great sounds and excitement of Bach's works. It was then that Schweitzer decided to become an organ builder, too. In time, his rebuilt organs became as famous as his concerts.

To share the burdens of others

At this same time, Schweitzer was working out his thoughts about Jesus Christ. His ideas often got him into trouble with religious leaders. He believed that Christ had made one mistake. Christ believed that if he sacrificed himself to the people who hurt him, the world would be a better place. Instead, Christ was killed and people had not changed at all. As Schweitzer said, "The world is full of suffering."

Schweitzer understood this suffering. He found it hard to be happy when he saw so many people hurt and hungry in

Opposite: Schweitzer the scholar is pictured at the peak of his powers. By this time, he knew that he had gifts in music, religion, and philosophy that few people could match.

26

This man suffers from the disease leprosy. Unless leprosy is treated in time, the patient's fingers and toes drop off, and white patches and huge, ugly sores appear on the person's skin. At Lambaréné, Schweitzer built a separate leper hospital to treat people who had this disease.

the world. Like Jesus, he felt that he should give his life to helping others.

Schweitzer takes action

Schweitzer decided to act on his beliefs. He decided he was going to make the world a better place for all people. It did not matter if he had to make sacrifices. He believed that everyone should share the burdens of the world. For him, the most important lesson Jesus taught was that only through love can people become one with God.

Schweitzer enjoyed being a preacher and teacher. But he wanted to do more than talk about love. He had worked with troubled children and homeless people during his years as a preacher. But even this was not enough.

At about this time, Schweitzer remembered a statue he had seen in the town of Colmar when he was a boy. The statue, by sculptor Frédéric Auguste Bartholdi, was of a sad but powerful African man. To young Albert, the statue showed all the sufferings of black people. He looked at the statue and felt he understood that suffering.

The needs of the Congo mission

And then, in 1904, Schweitzer read an article called "The needs of the Congo Mission." It was written by Dr. Alfred Boegner, who was president of the

Missionary Society of Paris. In the article, Boegner wrote about the terrible diseases hurting the Congo area. African men, women, and children needed doctors very badly. At that time, the Upper Congo belonged to France. It was known as French Equatorial Africa. Today this area is part of the Republic of Gabon.

Albert knew this was what he wanted to do. His search for a way to help the world was over. He decided to become a missionary doctor in Africa.

At first, his family and friends tried to stop him. They told him that he had a great future in Europe and that Africa was a dangerous place. But Albert had made up his mind.

Schweitzer turns to medicine

But Schweitzer was not a doctor. He was a musician and a student of religion. To help in Africa, he knew he would have to become a doctor. So he resigned his university job and, in 1905, began medical school. He was then thirty years old.

Schweitzer first met Hélène Bresslau during his years in medical school. Hélène's father, Harry Bresslau, taught history at the University of Strasbourg. He and Schweitzer had been close friends for years.

Hélène understood what Albert was trying to do. She wanted to help others, too. So she gave up her job as a social

Hélène Bresslau, the woman Albert Schweitzer would marry. She trained as a nurse to help him in his work. Soon after they married, they set off together for French Equatorial Africa to start their hospital.

worker to study nursing. As a nurse, she could help in Africa.

Between October and December of 1911, Schweitzer took the final tests for medical school. In a little over a year, he would be a fully qualified doctor. Already, he had written to Dr. Boegner and offered to work for the Missionary Society of Paris in Africa. Surprisingly, the missionary society turned down his offer. Some of its members did not agree with Schweitzer's ideas about religion. Schweitzer simply returned to his work.

The following year was a busy one. In the spring, Schweitzer began his work as an intern at a hospital in Paris. There, he

The Lambaréné hospital is located in what is now Gabon. This area was known as French Equatorial Africa when the Schweitzers arrived in 1913. To reach Lambaréné, the Schweitzers would first land by ship at Port Gentil. From there they traveled one hundred miles (160 km) up the Ogowé River. In the early days, supplies from Europe for the hospital took up to six months to arrive.

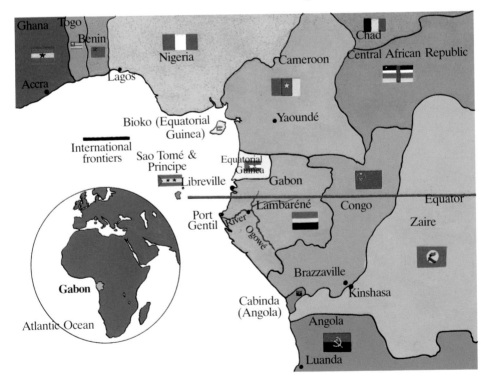

studied tropical medicine. And on June 18 of that year, Albert Schweitzer married Hélène Bresslau.

Doctor Albert Schweitzer

In 1913, Schweitzer became a doctor. He was now ready to begin his work in Africa. He was determined to get the missionary society to accept him.

He had already decided that he was going to raise his own money for his work. He wanted to raise enough to build a hospital at a place called Lambaréné. So he began calling on everyone he knew to get help for the mission. When he had enough money, he wrote to the missionary society again.

Surprisingly, some members of the group still did not trust Schweitzer. So he went to visit each one. Finally, they accepted him. But he had to promise not to preach his ideas to the people of Africa. He could work only as a doctor. Schweitzer agreed to these terms.

On March 21, 1913, Albert and Hélène took a train from the Günsbach railroad station to Paris. From there, a ship took them to Africa.

In Africa for the first time

Albert and Hélène Schweitzer landed at Lambaréné in April 1913. The climate in this part of Africa was hot and wet. The countryside did not seem welcoming.

When the Schweitzers first went to Africa, they were considered outstandingly brave. At the beginning of this century, the jungle was truly dangerous. With poor transportation and no medical facilities, there was a very high death rate among travelers to Africa.

A hollowed-out tree trunk serves as a boat, bringing patients and supplies along the Ogowé River to the hospital at Lambaréné. There was no road to the hospital until 1959.

Opposite: Often patients arrived so poorly nourished that they needed to be nursed back to health. Only then could Schweitzer and his team of doctors and nurses operate.

"We are really in Africa!" Schweitzer said happily. Beautiful plants grew everywhere, and tall trees climbed to the sky all around them. Many different kinds of birds circled above the boat as it floated along the river. Friendly people from the area waited on the shore to greet the Schweitzers. Already the doctor loved his new home.

The chicken-coop hospital

Lambaréné is an island in the middle of the Ogowé River. The nearest mission, at Andende, was a little way up this river, which was filled with crocodiles and hippopotamuses. No doctor or nurse had ever worked in this part of Africa.

At first, Schweitzer wanted to treat only very sick people because he needed time to build a proper hospital. But when he awoke the next day, patients were already lined up outside his door. The word had spread quickly: the new white doctor was here.

Seeing the people, the doctor changed his mind. He wanted to help these people right away. But first he had to have a place to work. The only empty building was a dirty chicken coop. The Schweitzers cleaned the coop as best they could and brought all of their equipment inside. This was to be their first jungle hospital.

At first, the Schweitzers only gave medicine and cleaned wounds. But soon,

Top: A rare photograph of the first hospital. Above: From the start, patients arrived with their families.

Schweitzer had to operate. Many of his patients had serious illnesses and injuries. He could not watch them suffer.

The new doctor found it difficult to communicate with his patients. But one of his very first patients solved this problem. The man, a native named Joseph Azowani, spoke French as well as his native language. With his help, Schweitzer could talk to his patients. Schweitzer asked Azowani to be his assistant. Azowani agreed and stayed with the doctor for fifty years.

Building a hospital

The Schweitzers soon began work on a new hospital. Many natives were glad to help. Together they built a hospital with clean, simple rooms. The building was ready by the end of the year.

To help the hospital run smoothly, Schweitzer made some rules. No spitting was allowed near the hospital. People waiting for care should not speak loudly. Patients and their families had to bring enough food for the whole day since not everyone could be treated in the morning.

The people obeyed these and all the other simple rules. They were happy to receive medical help. In return, they gave gifts of money and food to the hospital. This helped Schweitzer pay for more medicines, supplies, and other equipment for the hospital.

The Schweitzers are arrested

World War I started in 1914. France and Germany were on opposite sides of the fight. The Schweitzers were Germans working on French land. French officers arrested them on August 5, 1914. They could stay in their house, but they could not be with other people. Armed guards sent all the patients home.

Luckily, some of the officers knew about the Schweitzers' work and soon opened the clinic again. Albert and Hélène set to work once more and worked under these conditions for nearly three years. Then, in 1917, French soldiers sent them to a prison camp in southern France. After several months, they were released and went home to Günsbach.

This was how Schweitzer's jungle hospital looked in the early years. The thatch and bamboo roofs of these buildings did not last and did not protect patients from the weather. Corrugated-iron roofs later replaced them.

Opposite: Schweitzer works at his home in Günsbach, Alsace. The window looks out onto the foothills of the Vosges Mountains.

The Schweitzers despair

This was a sad time for the Schweitzers. The prison camp left both Albert and Hélène very tired and very ill. In time, Albert got better, but Hélène's health never fully returned. She was ill with tuberculosis for the rest of her life. Worse yet, Albert's mother had been killed during the war. A cavalry officer's horse had trampled her near Günsbach.

Schweitzer's life was at a low point. The war had really hurt him. He could not bear all the death and violence he had seen. The only ray of hope was the birth of his daughter, Rhena, on January 14, 1919. This was also Albert's birthday. After this, his energy slowly returned. He began to feel that the war had given him even more strength to fight for peace. He wanted more than ever to help people in need.

Schweitzer began to rebuild his life. He returned to his lectures and discovered that people still wanted to hear him speak. He started writing again and before long, he was rebuilding organs again, too.

And then he began to dream of returning to Africa. Hélène, with baby Rhena, could not return. The jungle climate would be too harsh for both of them. Only strong people could live there. It seemed they could never return.

Hélène told Albert to return to Africa without her. The people of Africa needed

In this photo from 1924, Albert Schweitzer sits on a log at Lambaréné. At his left and right are the first two doctors who came to assist him in his work.

him. She could make this sacrifice. She knew he had to go on alone.

Return to Africa

Albert Schweitzer was forty-nine years old when he returned to Lambaréné in 1924. He found the hospital in ruins. Some buildings had fallen down. Those still standing needed repair. With the help of the local people, Schweitzer rebuilt the hospital in his spare time.

Even the new hospital was not large enough to care for all the patients. Something had to be done. Schweitzer decided to move to a different location. He built a new clinic on land only two miles (3 km) away. It was a big project, but it separated him from the Missionary Society of Paris. Now he would be totally in charge of this hospital. He could even preach to the Africans about Jesus.

Patients moved into the new hospital in 1927. "For the first time since I began to work in Africa," Dr. Schweitzer said, "my patients were housed as human beings should be." After three years of hard work, Schweitzer felt he could return home to see his family.

A life of service

For the rest of his life, Schweitzer divided his time between Africa and Europe. While in Africa, he worked at the clinic in Lambaréné. In Europe, he gave concerts to raise money for the hospital. Sometimes he traveled to lecture or to accept awards. And as always, he spent time in Günsbach, visiting his family and writing.

People everywhere had respect for Albert. Many agreed when *Life* magazine called him "The Greatest Man in the World." Of course, he was not the first doctor to go to Africa. But Schweitzer used his fame wisely. With it, he inspired others to follow his way of living. His sacrifices gave others a good example.

Schweitzer's books also helped spread his beliefs. Through his books, he told millions of people about his respect for life. He told them of his dream for world

"In his prime, Schweitzer worked on a sixteen-hour schedule when he was on tour. His pace was fast and furious, but his immense reserves of energy were such that he could keep going on a minimum of food and sleep. After he had been working until four o'clock one morning a friend said to him, 'You cannot burn a candle at both ends.' But Schweitzer replied, 'Oh yes you can if the candle is long enough.'"
Everett Skillings

peace. Thousands of people — not just doctors and nurses — wanted to help. Albert Schweitzer had shown them how.

His great energy kept him working for fifty years. In that time, he quietly built up the hospital at Lambaréné. Unfortunately, Hélène's health kept her from helping at the hospital. She stayed in Europe and took care of little Rhena. But even from this distance, she supported her husband and the jungle hospital. In 1938, she went on a fund-raising tour of the United States. There she lectured about Albert's work in Africa.

World War II

World War II began in 1939. Schweitzer had felt it coming. Earlier that year, he bought as much medicine and equipment as his hospital could afford. He knew the war would slow or stop the supply ships. He was right. All too quickly, supplies began to run out. Luckily, Hélène's work in the United States began to help. Medicine and money sent by U.S. citizens kept the hospital going.

Still, hospital life was very hard during the war. Schweitzer's staff included only two other doctors and four nurses for the entire time. "What makes it so difficult to work in this country," Albert said, "is the terribly hot and moist climate. . . . I can stand the climate fairly well, but some of my co-workers suffer much from it."

Opposite: The hospital at Lambaréné was surrounded by a deep, tropical jungle. This was home to many kinds of wild animals. There were no roads, no shops, and none of the comforts of the Schweitzer home in Günsbach. The area was also very hot and humid. Many people could not stand this climate. But Albert Schweitzer's amazing strength never failed him. Even in his eighties, he would often work a sixteen-hour day after only four hours of sleep.

Lambaréné became a major hospital, helping up to one thousand patients a day. As it grew, Schweitzer himself organized all the building work. He also did his part of the day-to-day jobs. Schweitzer believed that no one was too important for the most humble tasks.

Daily life at Lambaréné

Life at Lambaréné went on. Schweitzer was now in his sixties and known worldwide. Yet by day, he still operated on patients and built rooms for his hospital. By night, he practiced Bach. Now, however, he used a special piano that the Paris Bach Society had sent him as a present. It had pedals like an organ.

Despite his fame, Schweitzer was still shy. He tried to keep his visits home to Europe a secret. As he wrote to one

French friend, "I suffer to be famous and try to avoid everything which draws more attention to me." He even asked people not to visit him in the jungle. He once said: "Please let me be as I am, someone who lives and works in silence."

Schweitzer did not always like the publicity. Above all, he wanted to protect his hospital. So anyone who did not approve of Lambaréné was not welcome. But he was careful not to turn everyone away. His hospital always needed money.

After many famines, Schweitzer created a large hospital vegetable garden. Year after year, the heavy rains washed away the fertile soil. Each year it had to be renewed. But in time, all the staff and over one thousand patients a day could be fed from this garden.

Schweitzer did much of the work at Lambaréné himself. For years — until he could afford a truck and a Jeep — this wheelbarrow was the hospital's only vehicle.

Those who did visit had to help. Two Americans spent several weeks at the Lambaréné hospital in 1947. They wrote, "We walked and talked, ate and worked, with Albert Schweitzer. . . . We were permitted to share the problems . . . the hopes . . . the dreams of this extraordinary jungle doctor."

The comical-looking hero

People who came to see Albert Schweitzer were often surprised. He was a comical-looking man. He almost never brushed his thick hair or mustache. The clothes he wore were old, baggy, and had usually been mended many times. In fact, his clothes sometimes seemed to be mostly patches. To top this off, Schweitzer usually wore an old sun helmet. Although one of his nurses once bought him a new hat, he did not wear it. He said that he liked the old one much better.

People knew Schweitzer by his clothes. Many also knew that he did not enjoy wearing fancy clothes. So few found it surprising that he wore the same old, black suit and clip-on bow tie to each meeting or ceremony.

"Anything I spend on myself," he once explained, "I can't spend on my Africans."

Schweitzer at work

Schweitzer often worked evenings in his little office. There, at an old termite-eaten table, he wrote late into the night. Sometimes, he worked on his mail. He received letters from all over the world, and he answered all of them.

Other times, he worked on his books. The finished chapters were tied together with string and piled on a shelf. If he still had work to do on a chapter, he would hang the pages on a nail on the wall. This is how he kept his work in order.

Even in his seventies, Schweitzer worked long hours. Yet he always had a lot of energy and was almost always in a good mood.

"One would never suppose that he had only three hours' sleep last night," one

"I opened the bundle. Here, for all I knew, was one of the most important books of our time. The sheets had been perforated at the top and were tied together by a string. But I gasped when I saw the kind of paper that had been used for the manuscript. There were sheets of every size and description. Dr. Schweitzer had written his book in longhand on the reverse side of miscellaneous papers. Some of them were outdated tax forms. . . . some came from old calendars. I couldn't even count the number of pages which were written on the reverse sides of letters."
Norman Cousins,
in Albert
Schweitzer's Mission

visitor said. "Last night he worked on his . . . papers until after midnight, spent two hours in the delivery room with the woman who was having her baby, and as usual got up at six."

Even Schweitzer was surprised by his own energy. "It is a grace," he said.

Reverence for life

Schweitzer wrote that the greatest good is to love all life. The greatest evil is to destroy life. He argued that all life is sacred. People are good only when they

Albert Schweitzer reads a letter from an admirer. Many people wrote to him. "My paperwork is killing me," he once complained. "Week by week the mail gets larger." Another time he joked, "Long after I am dead I feel I shall still be answering letters."

really believe this. Schweitzer planned his whole life around this idea. He called it "reverence for life."

This idea also applied to animals. Schweitzer loved animals — especially Africa's animals. The local people often asked him to help their sick animals, and he had many pets of his own.

Among these pets were a pelican, a pig, and a porcupine that danced when he played the piano. Dogs followed him all around the hospital yard, wagging their tails. In the evenings he fed a shy pet owl

Every night Schweitzer would play Bach on his piano. This brought him great joy and peace. It also served as practice for the many concerts he gave in Europe.

bits of meat. And monkeys climbed on all the porches.

Schweitzer once said that as many as 250 sheep and goats lived at the clinic. "They are not killed. They will die a natural death. We have a pelican which lodges in a tree opposite my room. His friends are a goat and its child." Even dogs and monkeys lived together. This way of life was important to Schweitzer.

Schweitzer's sick pelican

The hospital at Lambaréné had many rooms and huts for sick people. But sick animals had space at the hospital, too. Schweitzer built stables for these patients. He even operated on animals that needed special help.

One assistant did not understand Schweitzer's idea of reverence for life. He did not approve of all the animals. There were so many sick people who needed care.

Then one day, the assistant saw that Schweitzer's pelican had been wounded. He sent word to Schweitzer. The doctor treated all his human patients before he came to see the pelican. The assistant was surprised. Schweitzer explained that the sick people at Lambaréné came first.

In 1960, a news reporter asked Schweitzer to explain his beliefs about life. Schweitzer simply answered: "All that I have to say to the world and to

Schweitzer walks with his pelican Parsifal. By day it swam in the river or flew into the jungle. But each night it returned. Schweitzer wrote a book, supposedly in the pelican's own words, in which Parsifal says, "I swore that the doctor would not easily shake me off."

mankind is contained in the notion, reverence for life."

Schweitzer came to believe that people should be vegetarians. Vegetarians are people who do not eat meat. By becoming vegetarians, people would show respect for animal life. He said: "The great problem whether we ought to kill and eat animals is . . . becoming clear to us. There is much to be said against it." Schweitzer only wished that he had become a vegetarian earlier in life.

"We have invented many things, but we have not mastered the creation of life. We cannot even create an insect."

Albert Schweitzer

Every day after dinner, Schweitzer would fill his pockets with crusts and go to the antelope pen, where the animals would rush to him.

Sick people crowd Schweitzer's hospital. They brought their families and often even their livestock with them. The people stayed on the hospital grounds until their sick ones were healed.

The people of Africa

Living in French Equatorial Africa, Schweitzer came to love the African people. These people had very hard lives, yet most were very kind and showed great respect for each other.

The doctor especially liked a schoolmaster named Oyembo. Oyembo taught in the Lambaréné school. Schweitzer thought Oyembo was one of the finest men he knew. Oyembo was smart, kind, and modest. Schweitzer once said that "there was something so refined about [Oyembo] that one almost felt shy in his presence."

But Schweitzer did not feel that he always acted as refined as Oyembo did. Sometimes he even lost his temper. He remembered the way his assistants acted when this happened. "They quietly went about their work, and remained as friendly as if they had never had to endure our probably ... excessive abuse." Schweitzer knew he was learning much from his time in Africa.

Justice in the jungle

Schweitzer also had respect for the laws of the African people. Tribal chiefs decided what was right and wrong.

But not all Europeans were as respectful of these laws as Schweitzer was. Some tried to make their own laws in Africa. Many of these Europeans did not know the African people and did not speak their language. They did not understand a lifestyle so different from their own.

Schweitzer did not like many of the Europeans who came to live in Africa. He felt that most of these settlers were there only to make money. They really did not love Africa or its people.

Schweitzer especially disliked the slave trade that the white Europeans had begun

Albert and Hélène Schweitzer together at Lambaréné in 1957, shortly before her death. Albert appreciated her presence: "She keeps going all day long and her help is very precious."

centuries earlier. Through this system, the traders had shipped black Africans to America and the West Indies. Some traders even bribed black leaders to sell their own people. Often members of a black family never saw each other again once they were sold.

The slave trade lasted many years. When it ended, America had received about twelve million black slaves. Probably another two million Africans died on the ships that carried them across the Atlantic Ocean.

Taking advantage of Africa

The slave trade finally fell off in the late 1800s. Yet even in the 1900s, Schweitzer saw that white people did not treat black people fairly. In 1928 he wrote an article called "The Relations of the White and Colored Races." In it, he said that white settlers had destroyed the African way of life. They had taken freedom away from the black people.

Schweitzer was certain that most Europeans did not respect Africans. White settlers had taken the best land for their cities. They forced villagers out of their homes. After that, the Europeans did not even provide education for the Africans. This made Schweitzer angry. The white settlers had promised schools for the African people. But they sent only a few teachers to the colonies.

Albert Schweitzer listens to organ music in a Swedish church.

A man of the world

Albert Schweitzer also kept his eyes on world problems. The invention of the atomic bomb was one thing that worried him very much. Schweitzer knew that even testing such weapons was dangerous because it put harmful radioactive material into the air.

The powerful countries would not listen to Schweitzer or anyone else who spoke out against the bomb. They continued to build nuclear weapons.

Some people even began to criticize Schweitzer for his opinions. This hurt the doctor but did not change his mind.

The Nobel Prize

In 1952, seventy-seven-year-old Albert Schweitzer won the Nobel Peace Prize. At once, he used the prize money to build a new section for his hospital at Lambaréné. This section was built just to care for patients with leprosy.

But it was not until a year later that Schweitzer actually traveled to Norway to accept his award. In his speech, he talked about world peace. He said he spoke for the millions of people who were afraid of another war. He also spoke against officials who did not work toward peace. He said: "Let those who hold the fates of peoples in their hands be careful to avoid everything which may worsen our situation."

Schweitzer sometimes felt that the end of the human race was in sight. Weak people had too many powerful weapons. Schweitzer felt that people had only one real choice. They had to work toward becoming "simpler, more truthful, purer, more peace-loving, meeker, kinder, more sympathetic" to all living things.

Schweitzer works for peace

Schweitzer's Nobel Peace Prize speech echoed the beliefs by which he lived.

Many of the world's universities — Edinburgh, Oxford, Tübingen, Yale, Cambridge — showered honors on Schweitzer.

These ideas could change the future of humankind. But they could affect the future of the earth, too. For Schweitzer knew that nuclear weapons could destroy more than people. They could destroy all forms of life on earth.

Schweitzer had another idea. He said that governments had to learn to trust each other. Only through trusting each other could the countries of the world agree to ban nuclear weapons. But the governments could not do all this work alone. People had to help. They had to speak out against atomic weapons. Schweitzer believed that a "surge of public opinion in the East and in the West condemning atomic weapons" was the only way to avoid nuclear war.

Abolishing nuclear weapons

Finally, some of the world's most powerful countries began to listen to people such as Schweitzer. They agreed to stop nuclear testing. Schweitzer saw this agreement as only a beginning. The weapons that already existed had to be destroyed. But governments were slow to do this.

Schweitzer again spoke about the need for trust. "One government can be replaced by another government," he said, "but the people remain and their will is decisive. The people themselves must take a stand." Schweitzer believed that if people really wanted peace, they would have to help control their governments.

Could people really make a difference? Schweitzer thought so. He said that people would have to believe in the need for peace and trust. Above all, they must learn to respect all life. When individuals believed in these things, they could influence their governments. But, as Schweitzer pointed out, "The miracle must happen in us before it can happen in the world."

Schweitzer taught respect. "The only way out of today's misery is for people to become worthy of each other's trust," he declared.

The last journey to Lambaréné

In his later years, Schweitzer spent much time traveling to different countries. Wherever he went, however, he missed his hospital. During his last visit to

Europe, Schweitzer played the organ for a friend one evening. The music reminded him of Lambaréné. It was time to return.

Albert Schweitzer made his final journey to Lambaréné in 1959. He wanted to spend the rest of his life there. He also wanted to be buried beside Hélène, who had died in 1957.

Schweitzer was now well into his eighties, but his life went on as it always had. He continued to work on and run the hospital. He wrote letters and books, fed the animals, and greeted visitors. And, as always, he played his beloved Bach. Albert Schweitzer led a simple, quiet life. He died just as he had lived on September 4, 1965. He was ninety years old.

Lambaréné: The graves of Albert and Hélène Schweitzer are marked by simple wooden crosses.

Huge crowds of men, women, and children came to say good-bye to the jungle doctor. One worker described how one morning she "woke at six o'clock to the singing of children and adults; for half an hour they sang, expressing their love and gratitude. . . . I thought of the doctor, how this would touch him in his soul. Once a native said to him, 'When you die we will have a tom-tom of a week to mourn you.' The doctor jokingly replied, 'Fortunately, I won't hear it.'"

To find out more . . .

Organizations

The organizations listed below can help you learn more about Albert Schweitzer, current medical and health issues, or careers in medicine. Your local health department is also a good place to start to find out more about specific health problems. Check your phone book for the department's address. When you write to any of these organizations, be sure to tell them exactly what you want to know. Also include your name, address, and age.

Albert Schweitzer Center
Hurlburt Road, R.D. 1, Box 7
Great Barrington, MA 01230

Albert Schweitzer Fellowship
866 United Nations Plaza
New York, NY 10017

American Medical Association
Information Center
515 N. State Street
Chicago, IL 60610

American Nurses' Association
2420 Pershing Road
Kansas City, MO 64108

Books

About Albert Schweitzer —

Days with Albert Schweitzer: A Lambaréné Landscape. Frederick
    Franck (Henry Holt)
Dr. Schweitzer of Lambaréné. Norman Cousins (Dutton)
The Value of Dedication: The Story of Albert Schweitzer.
    Spencer Johnson (Oak Tree)

About Africa —

Africa. Simon Baynham (Franklin Watts)
Africa. Francene Sabin (Troll)
Famine in Africa. Lloyd Timberlake (Franklin Watts)
The Scramble for Africa. Trevor Rowell (David & Charles)

About Composers and Music —

Great Composers and Their Music. Audrey J. Adair (Prentice Hall)
Lives of Great Composers. Ian Woodward (Merry Thoughts)
More Stories of Composers for Young Musicians. Catherine W.
  Kendall (Toadwood)
Stories of Composers for Young Musicians. Catherine W. Kendall
  (Toadwood)
You Can Be a Musician and a Missionary, Too. Renee Kent; edited by
  Cindy McClain (Woman's Missionary Union)

About World Peace and Peacemakers —

Peace Is . . . Maxine M. Roberson (Standard Publishing)
Peace Porridge. Marjie Douglis (Bethel)
A Peaceable Warrior. Marguerite Murray (Macmillan)
Prepare for Peace, Part I. Ruth Obold (Faith & Life)
Prepare for Peace, Part II. Ruth Obold (Faith & Life)

Magazines

The magazines listed below may give you more information about
health, medicine, and events occurring around the world. Check
your library to see if they have these magazines. You can also
write to the addresses listed to get information about subscribing.

Children's Digest
P.O. Box 10003
Des Moines, Iowa   50340

Faces
20 Grove Street
Peterborough, New Hampshire 03458

Jack and Jill
P.O. Box 10003
Des Moines, Iowa   50340

Owl
(in Canada)
56 The Esplanade, Suite 304
Toronto, Ontario M5E 1A7
Canada

(in the United States)
P.O. Box 11314
Des Moines, Iowa 50340

The Small Street Journal
405 East Colorado Avenue
Colorado Springs, Colorado   80903

3-2-1 Contact
P.O. Box 53051
Boulder, Colorado 80322-3051

List of new words

Alsace
> An area in eastern France along the Rhine River. Alsace has changed hands between France and Germany many times.

anesthetic
> A substance that stops feeling and allows a doctor to operate without causing pain to the patient. A local anesthetic numbs only the area that is hurt. A general anesthetic puts the patient to sleep.

Bach, Johann Sebastian (1685-1750)
> A European organist and composer. Bach spent most of his life in Germany. He wrote many musical masterpieces and is considered one of the greatest composers of all time.

French Equatorial Africa
> A part of central Africa that once belonged entirely to the French government. This area included several colonies.

Gabon, Republic of
> An area in western central Africa that was colonized by the

French in 1839. It became part of the Congo in 1888. The area received its freedom in 1960, but it is still part of the French community of states.

Lambaréné
An island in central Africa where Albert Schweitzer built his first hospital. The island lies in Africa's huge Ogowé River.

leprosy
A disease in humans that attacks mainly the skin and nervous system. People who have leprosy often lose feeling in the diseased parts of their bodies. They may also develop blotchy, lumpy skin. In serious cases, fingers and toes may fall off. Doctors can now cure leprosy with drugs. About twelve million people in the world still suffer from this disease today. It is also known as Hansen's disease.

malaria
A disease caused by the bite of a certain kind of mosquito. The symptoms are fever and chills. Malaria can spread easily and is hard to cure. Patients have to take medicine for a long time.

Mendelssohn, Felix (1809-1847)
A famous German composer. His beautiful *Songs Without Words* helped to inspire the young Albert Schweitzer to play serious music.

missionary
A person sent by a religious group to help in a foreign country. Most missionaries take religious vows.

Nobel Prizes
Yearly awards given for work in certain areas. Nobel Prizes are awarded in chemistry, physics, economics, medicine, and literature, and for promoting peace. Albert Schweitzer was awarded the Nobel Peace Prize in 1952.

nuclear arms
Dangerous weapons that get their power from nuclear energy. This is the energy that is released when atoms are broken apart or forced together.

Oslo
The capital city of Norway. Oslo is primarily a seaport. Albert Schweitzer gave his acceptance speech for the Nobel Peace Prize in this city.

philosophy
The study of knowledge and wisdom. Those who study or teach philosophy look at everything that humankind has ever learned.

publicity
Public attention; also, information that is spread as a means of gaining public attention.

respect
To hold someone in high regard; to treat someone with dignity.

reverence
A feeling of deep honor and respect for someone or something. Albert Schweitzer believed in an idea that he called "reverence for life." This was the idea that all life is sacred and that to destroy life of any kind is wrong.

sleeping sickness
Another name for a disease caused by the bite of the tsetse fly. This sickness occurs mainly in tropical climates. Its symptoms are fever, tiredness, and weak muscles.

Strasbourg
A seaport in northeastern France. Albert Schweitzer attended the University of Strasbourg.

theology

The study of religion, and especially of God and his teachings.

vegetarian

A person who does not eat meat or meat products.

vineyard

Land that is used for growing grapes. There are many fine vineyards in the Alsace region of France.

Widor, Charles-Marie (1845-1937)

A French organist and composer, born in Lyons, France. Widor became the organist at St. Sulpice in Paris in 1869. He composed symphonies and many other works for the organ.

witch doctor

A person who practices a kind of primitive medicine. Witch doctors use magic and potions to cure patients. African people used only witch doctors until the arrival of modern medicine.

Important dates

1875   **January 14** — Albert Schweitzer is born in Kaysersberg, Upper Alsace.
Summer — The Schweitzers move to Günsbach.

1880   Schweitzer begins playing the piano and organ.

1884   At the age of nine, Schweitzer begins playing the organ for services in his father's church.

1885   Schweitzer goes to secondary school at Mülhausen.

1890   Schweitzer begins studying music under Eugen Münch.

1893   **October** — Schweitzer studies organ under Charles-Marie Widor in Paris.

November — He enters the University of Strasbourg to study theology and philosophy.

1899   **August** — Schweitzer earns his degree in philosophy from the University of Strasbourg.
December — He becomes pastor of St. Nicholas Church in Strasbourg.

1900   Schweitzer earns a degree in theology.

1904   Schweitzer decides to become a medical missionary.

1905   Schweitzer resigns from his college and begins training as a doctor of medicine at Strasbourg.

1911   Schweitzer finishes his medical studies.
To raise money for his examination fee, he begins giving concerts. He also raises money to build a hospital in central Africa.

1912   **June 18** — Schweitzer marries Hélène Bresslau.

1913   Schweitzer becomes a doctor.
The Schweitzers sail for Africa and open a jungle hospital at Lambaréné.

1914   World War I begins. French authorities arrest the Schweitzers because they are German subjects.

1916   **July** — Schweitzer's mother dies.

1917   The Schweitzers are taken to France as prisoners of war.

1918   The Schweitzers are released from a French prison camp and return to Günsbach.
November 11 — World War I ends.

1919 January 14 — The Schweitzers' daughter, Rhena, is born.

1920 Schweitzer begins lecturing and giving organ concerts so that he can raise enough money to return to Lambaréné.

1924 Schweitzer reaches Lambaréné and finds it in ruins. Hélène and Rhena remain in Europe for health reasons.

1927-1939 Schweitzer frequently visits Europe to be with his family and to raise money for the hospital.

1932 In a speech at Frankfurt, Germany, Schweitzer warns of the dangers of Nazism and a second world war.

1939 September 1 — World War II begins. Schweitzer knows the danger in Europe and no longer visits. Hélène joins him in Africa in 1941.

1950-1952 Schweitzer tours many countries, giving concerts and speaking out against nuclear weapons.

1952 Schweitzer is awarded the Nobel Peace Prize. He uses the money to build a village for three hundred people with leprosy.

1957 Hélène Schweitzer dies in Zurich, Switzerland, and is buried at Lambaréné.

1965 September 4 — Schweitzer dies at Lambaréné. He is buried in a simple wooden coffin next to his wife.

1976 The hospital at Lambaréné is rebuilt because buildings have become too old and shabby for patient care.

1981 January — A modern hospital opens at Lambaréné.

Index

Africa: climate of 5, 31, 36, 41; original natives of 51, 52; settlement of 51
Alsace 10, 11, 17, 22
Andende 32
Azowani, Joseph 34

Bach, Johann Sebastian 23, 25, 26, 42
Bartholdi, Frédéric Auguste 28
Boegner, Alfred 28-29, 30
Brahms, Johannes 21
Bresslau, Harry 29
Bresslau, Hélène (Schweitzer) 29-30, 31, 35, 36, 38, 41, 59

Colmar 28
Congo 29

European settlers in Africa 51, 52

French Equatorial Africa 29

Gabon, Republic of 9, 10, 29
Günsbach 11, 16, 17, 19, 35

Kaysersberg 10-11

Lambaréné 6, 7-8, 9, 31, 32, 33, 34, 38-39, 41, 44, 48, 55
leprosy 5, 55
Life 10, 39

malaria 5
Mendelssohn, Felix 21
Missionary Society of Paris 29, 30, 31, 39
Mülhausen 18
Münch, Eugen 20-21

"The needs of the Congo Mission" 28
New York Times 10
Nobel Peace Prize 55
nuclear weapons 54, 56-57

Oyembo 50-51

Paris Bach Society 25, 42

reverence for life 16, 46-47

Schweitzer, Adéle (mother) 11, 36
Schweitzer, Albert: arrest of 35; becomes a doctor 29-31; birth and childhood of 10-22, 25; death of 59; education of 11-13, 17-18, 19-21, 22-24, 29, 30; and fame 39, 42-44; as "The Greatest Man in the World" 10, 39; life in Mülhausen of 18-21; marriage of 31; as musician 11-13, 19-21, 23, 25-26, 39, 42; and the Nobel Peace Prize 55; and nuclear weapons 54, 56-57; as organ builder 26, 36; as preacher 24-25; in prison camp 35, 36; religious ideas of 21-22, 26, 31, 39; and studies in Berlin 24; and studies in Paris 23, 24; as teacher 25; as vegetarian 49; as writer 25, 36, 39, 45
Schweitzer, Hélène (*see* Bresslau, Hélène)
Schweitzer, Louis (father) 11
Schweitzer, Louis (great-uncle) 18
Schweitzer, Rhena 36
Schweitzer, Sophie 18, 19
slave trade 51, 52
sleeping sickness 5
Strasbourg 24

United Nations Commission on Human Rights 10
University of Strasbourg 23-24, 25, 29
Upper Congo 29

Widor, Charles-Marie 23, 25-26
witch doctors 8
world wars 7, 35, 41

DATE DUE

MAR 30 1992			
APR 6 1992			

Lantier, Patricia
Albert Schweitzer